The Hummel
Thank You Book

with authentic Hummel pictures

ars edition

I feel the earth more sunward,
I join the great march onward,
And take, by faith, while living,
My freehold of thanksgiving.

John Greenleaf Whittier

There lies also love, in that
one accepts a good deed.

Julius Wolff

There is in the world seldom
a more beautiful excess
than that of thankfulness.

Jean de la Bruyère

O Lord, that lends me life,
Lend me a heart replete with
thankfulness!
For thou hast given me in this
beauteous face a world of
earthly blessing to my soul.

Shakespeare

We are only rich
in what we give
and poor only through
what we refuse.

Madame Swetchine

He who allows his day to pass by
without practicing generosity
and enjoying life's pleasures
is like a blacksmith's bellows –
he breathes but does not live.

Sanskrit proverb

You may give without loving –
but you can't love without giving.

Folk saying

Express gratitude generously
and sincerely;
receive gratitude humbly
and graciously;
expect gratitude rarely, if ever.

William Arthur Ward

Be grateful for what you have,
not regretful for what you haven't.

Folk saying

A gift, though small, is welcome.

Homer

Who does not thank for little
will not thank for much.

Estonian proverb

It's wiser being good than bad;
It's safer to be meek than fierce;
It's fitter being sane than mad.
My own hope is, a sun will pierce
The thickest cloud earth ever stretched;
That, after Last, returns the First,
Though a wide compass round be fetched;
That what began best can't end worst,
Nor what God blessed once, prove accurst.

Robert Browning

If one person has something
very precious to thank another for,
this thanks should remain
a secret between the two of them.

Rainer Maria Rilke

May kindness be repaid to him
who does a kindness.

Babylonian proverb

Who pleasure gives, shall joy receive.

Benjamin Franklin

The only true happiness comes
from squandering ourselves
for a purpose.

John Mason Brown

One always experiences the greatest joy
where one has least expected it.

Antoine de Saint-Exupéry

I give thee thanks in part of
thy deserts
And will with deeds requite
thy gentleness.

Shakespeare

By appreciation we make excellence
in others our own property.

Voltaire

The more joy we have,
the more nearly perfect we are.

Baruch Spinoza

Small service is true service
while it lasts!
Of humblest friends, bright creature,
scorn not one;
The daisy, by the shadow
that it casts,
Protects the lingering dewdrop
from the sun.

William Wordsworth

One may refuse a request,
but one may never refuse thanks,
or take it in a cold and conventional way,
which is the same thing.

Friedrich Nietzsche

O wad some Pow'r the giftie gie us
To see oursels as others see us!
It wad frae mony a blunder free us
And foolish notion.

Robert Burns

Little drops of water,
little grains of sand
make the mighty ocean,
and the pleasant land
So the little minutes,
humble though they be
Make the mighty ages
of eternity.

Little deeds of kindness,
little words of love,
Help to make earth happy,
like the heaven above.

Julia Carney

Tell part of a person's praise
in his presence and all of it
in his absence.

The Talmud

Be both a speaker of words
and a doer of deeds.

Homer

Praise makes good men better
and bad men worse.

Thomas Fuller

Heaven gave mankind three things
to counter the hardships of life:
Hope, Sleep and Laughter.

Immanuel Kant

Life was meant to be lived,
and curiosity must be kept alive.
One must never, for whatever reason,
turn his back on life.

Eleanor Roosevelt

Who finds a faithful friend
finds a treasure.

Ecclesiasticus

The wise man does not lay up treasure.
The more he gives to others,
the more he has for his own.

Lao-tse

When you drink from the stream,
remember the spring.

Chinese proverb

When the voices of children
are heard on the green
And laughing is heard on the hill,
My heart is at rest within my breast
And every thing else is still.

Then come home my children,
the sun is gone down
And the dews of night arise
Come come leave off play,
and let us away
Till the morning appears in the skies.

William Blake

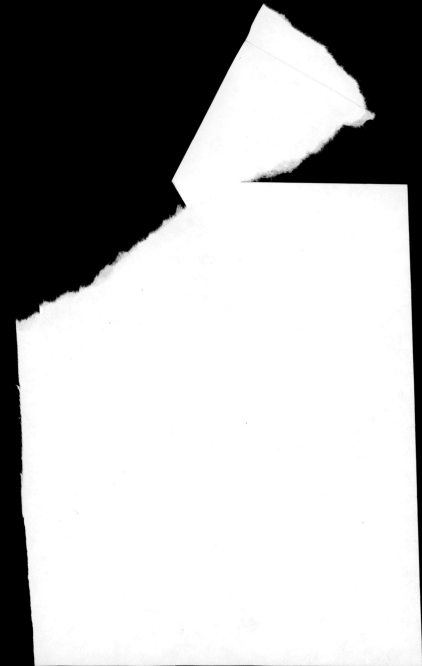

We at Ars Edition hope this little book has brought
you pleasure. The pages of this collector's edition
are folded back-to-back, in a style known as
Japanese binding. You may wish to collect all these
beautiful Hummel books:

> The Hummel Friendship Book
> The Hummel Thank You Book
> The Hummel Get Well Book
> The Hummel Birthday Book

For the store nearest you which carries our Hummel
books, please write us.

ars edition *inc.*

"The Original Hummel People"

70 Air Park Drive, Ronkonkoma, NY 11779

© 1983 ars edition · all rights reserved
arranged and edited by Jonathan Roth
printed in West Germany · ISBN 0-86724-052-0